WORDPRESS

Simple WordPress Guide to Creating an Attractive Website or Blog, from Scratch, Step-by-step.

Felix Alvaro

Acknowledgments

Firstly, I would like to thank God for giving us the knowledge and inspiration to put this informative book together. I also want to thank my partner Silvia, my parents and younger brothers for their support and my right-hand man Fabian for his motivation. Finally, I would like to thank Michelle for her contribution in the creation of this book.

Table of Contents

Introduction

Hello there! Thanks for acquiring this eBook. You have made a great decision and a huge investment in your skills as a developer! The information in this eBook will guide you away from the struggles of creating a website through WordPress, as it did for me. I know the feeling of wanting to share your ideas with the world but finding difficulty -or losing motivation- with navigating top platforms such as WordPress, or knowing where to get started all together. This eBook will remove those feelings of uncertainty, and will provide you with a sense of direction that you have been missing in creating your site. My name is Felix, I'm an Online Marketer and Entrepreneur, and I will teach you, with proven steps, how to create your own blog or website without a single mishap or overwhelming lecture. I guarantee it will be easy and quick to grasp.

I myself have created web pages before using different software and have found WordPress to be the easiest, safest and fastest to learn. For instance, I constructed all the main parts of a website for one of my businesses in just 2 days. It saved me a lot of time and money, where, through different platforms, that may not have been the case. You will have the same experience, as you learn to develop a remarkable blog/website and gain the skill to create your own brand and design without having to spend money hiring a web designer.

In the US, hiring a Web-designer costs between $60-$200 per hour, this book didn't cost you even a fraction of that amount, but will provide you with tremendous value and a skill you get to keep and develop. Many self-taught designers are making their way to the web every day and I promise that this book will lead you on that track. The knowledge that you will gain is enough to remove all self-doubts, fears, and even dispel procrastination, by inspiring you to get started right away.

If you have any questions or doubts whilst reading this book, feel free to drop me an email and I will do my best to get back to you promptly. You can find my contact information in the last page of this book. Don't keep your personal blog or website waiting any longer! Now is the time to invest in yourself and invest in your future. Get ready to attain a distinctive skill that many wish they had. A grand amount of information awaits your viewing. Let us get to it!

In the first chapter, I will give you a better understanding of how WordPress works, and the benefits of using such a powerful tool. I will also be breaking-down the two different platforms that they have available, and the benefits that they bring to you and me.

Let's get to it!

Chapter One: Understanding WordPress

In this chapter, I will discuss the reasons why WordPress is so tremendously popular today, I will reveal the two platforms that they have available, and I will also provide you with a brief overview of everything you need to know to get started right away.

For 2015, WordPress is currently the most popular platform when it comes to building your website or blog, and there are clearly good reasons for this.

For starters, WordPress is designed to be extremely user friendly, and is, without a doubt, the most 'beginner-friendly' platform. If we look back to when people created websites the old-fashioned way using HTML (coding), CSS, or even flash, it was rather difficult to create a properly functioning website. Those who were not familiar with coding would have to spend hours-upon-hours studying coding and going through numerous books. This idea holds no appeal; hence the reason why countless people today are still uncomfortable or even terrified with the thought of creating a website.

What differentiates WordPress, is the use of plugin architecture, and a template system that is already fully constructed. A developer like yourself can easily install themes, plugins, and widgets, out of a massive selection, whilst still creating and designing a website that is very unique to you and to your service.

The websites or blogs created through WordPress are also mobile-friendly, allowing users to visit your website either through their computer-screen, or their mobile device. While still maintaining an enjoyable and suitable experience, whether that is a 'compact' version of your website for easier access on the go, or a more in-depth layout suitable for the comfort of your visitor's home or office.

WordPress goes above and beyond its competition! In 2015, there were over 50,000 websites created daily using the spectacular structures offered by WordPress, which brings the platform to own 23% of all *globally* used websites. How did their competitors fair? Joomla earned 6.8% of the market while Drupal currently holds 5%. A significant gap in market-share!

Before we move any further, I want to take the time to explain that there are two different options when creating a blog or website, and these can be easily mistaken if not explained.

1. WordPress.com

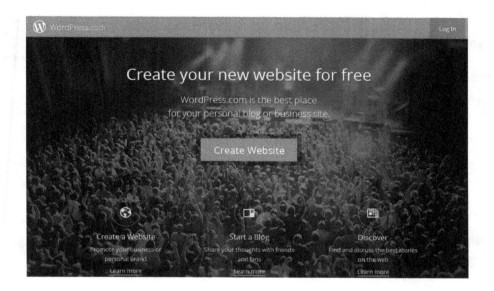

Firstly, we have 'Wordpress.com.' Wordpress.com is a commercial website that enables us to host a blog or website free of charge with the basic version. The platform your site will operate on is already fully constructed and has a completely updated security system. In summary, it is a basic, 'systemized' host server where you are required to sign-up and decide on a name for your blog. Since this is an already pre-designed option there is quite a lot of restriction that follows; however, you can upgrade to get more usability out of this selection. Of course, nothing comes free, so be aware that upgrades will come at a very high price!

2. WordPress.org

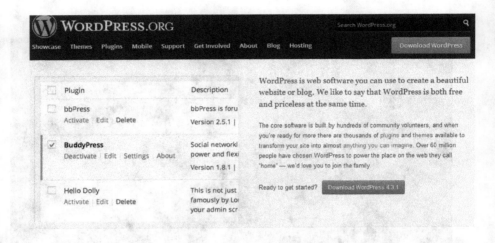

Secondly, we have 'WordPress.org.' WordPress.org consists of software that you can use to build a fully-customizable website. The software can be downloaded for free. Afterwards, you can synchronize it with a domain and a hosting server, which you must purchase from a hosting company (this will be broken down further on, do not worry!). Then we get the freedom to completely modify it to our tastes.

I like to use a short metaphor to illustrate the benefits of each. For example, imagine you want to buy a new home. There are two routes you can take:

1. **You buy a house that is already built**
2. **You buy land and build everything from the ground-up**

Note: To understand the bigger picture, a majority of the time it is cheaper to build your own home in comparison to buying a house that is already built. Although it depends on where you live and the factors that go into purchasing properties.

There are always pros and cons with every choice and these have been laid out for you.

If You Buy a Home That is <u>Already-Built</u> You Will Benefit From:

- Only needing to purchase it
- Make a few decorative changes to suit your tastes since everything else has been pre-designed before purchase

However, the negatives are:

- You would pay more. It is likely the seller is selling it for more than what they paid
- Limiting alterations
- Expensive to upgrade (knock walls, expand kitchen, etc.)
- Not 100% what you originally pictured when purchasing a home

With Building <u>From-Scratch</u> You Will Benefit From:

- Creating exactly what you want
- Easier on the wallet
- No limits as to what you can do

The downside:

- Most likely you would be doing the majority of the work
- Time consuming
- Being involved in every step of the building process, with no down time

That is how one could compare WordPress.com and WordPress.org.

The choice is yours as to whether you want to use WordPress.com or WordPress.org. You can either pay more with using WordPress.com that has limitations on what was already completed for you. Or you can pay less with WordPress.org which allows full control and responsibility in creating the idea you want to present.

Notably, my preference is with WordPress.org, and that is the vehicle we will observe throughout this book. While it does involve more responsibility, this does not mean it will be difficult to use. As a matter of fact, as mentioned at the start of the book, it does not require one to have a high skill level in developing. It simply requires the skill to use a PC, and to follow the instructions I have laid out in this book. This book will provide you with a stress-free guide to creating an exceedingly professional, high- quality website or blog.

This chapter has given you an understanding of WordPress, an overview of how it operates, as well as the differences between WordPress.org and Wordpress.com. In the next chapter, we will begin working on your site. I am going to take you through the first steps, which are giving your website an Identity and an existence by creating a domain name and setting up a hosting server.

Let's get to it...

Chapter Two: Creating an Identity and Existence for the Website

Now that you understand a little bit about the power, benefits, and the usability of WordPress, we will now begin moving into some action. In this chapter, you will gain the skills to give your website a professional domain name, get it live on the web, as well as a few key tips for optimizing your search-engine ranking in the process.

The first step to take for your website is to get a domain name and a hosting server.

Please Note: If you already have a domain and hosting server you may skip to Chapter 3 where I will discuss the installation of WordPress.

Just like humans, all websites also need a residence. For instance, if you wanted to invite people to visit your home, you would have to provide them with an address. With that address, they would then be able to locate your house. The same concept applies to websites. Websites use domains, which are simply the web addresses people search on the internet. Those addresses will then link the website to the viewer's web browser. For example, 'www.yournamehere.com'would be your domain. I'm sure you understand the point!

Finally, we will get you a hosting server that will connect your website to the world-wide-web (the internet). The hosting server basically allows you to 'hire' digital space for your website, and allows other people on the internet to see your site.

With numerous options for setting up both, I will recommend those which I believe to be the best. Some sites that offer these services certainly cause confusion, and I wish to avoid that. Here I present options which I know offer good services with a competitive price.

<u>For the attainment of a domain name and host server I would recommend using a company called:</u>

BLUEHOST (www.bluehost.com)

They are very affordable and quite often offer discounts on your first domain names and second domain names. Most importantly, the company is a one-stop shop for the purchase of your domain and the hosting server. For example, when I began writing this section, Bluehost offered a special package consisting of the purchase of your host server for $3.49 per month, with the domain name for free.

basic

normally $7.99

$3.49* per month

select

websites	1
website space	50 GB
bandwidth	unmetered
performance	Standard
included domains	1
parked domains	5
sub domains	25
email accounts	5
email storage	100 MB per account
marketing offers	—

select

To add a professional twist, they also throw in personal email accounts for your website (for example yourname@yourbusiness.com) which will vastly boost your professionalism and increase your credibility. These business-like email accounts can also be synchronized with your Gmail or outlook accounts and you can set-up up to 5 accounts with the basic package!

When choosing a hosting plan, the most common hosting options you will see from the majority of hosts are the following:

- Shared hosting
- Pro web hosting
- VPS hosting
- Dedicated hosting

I understand that at first glance that can be a bit overwhelming. Let us focus on the packages I deem most important for someone building their first website, that is choosing between a 'Shared' or a 'Dedicated' hosting service plan.

I will highlight some of the main differences between the two and what you should be taking into consideration:

- You get more bandwidth (disk-space) with the dedicated server
- The dedicated server requires technical skills for maintenance and security
- The dedicated server costs a lot more as it is only one website on the server
- Shared server comes with firewalls, security applications and programs for you
- Shared servers are much cheaper
- Shared servers may slow down the response and loading time due to higher bandwidth requirement from one of the users
- Shared server means you *share* the space with other sites

As always, there are pros and cons with both servers. However, I would always recommend going with a shared server from a reputable host (like bluehost.com). It is more cost-efficient, requires a lot less work and technical ability, plus you and your visitors can still have a great browsing experience. Bluehost also offers better packages of the shared server where you can have an even higher quality server for a few extra pounds/dollars.

I urge following the links below if you want more information about the different hosting services:

https://my.bluehost.com/cgi/help/started

https://my.bluehost.com/cgi/help/141

Another good service provider is Siteground (www.siteground.com).

Siteground also offers the package of both domain names and the hosting server for sometimes an even cheaper price than Bluehost. I advise checking them out as well if you wish to have something to compare with.

There are also other service providers out there, such as Godaddy.com. I would mainly focus on the sites I have mentioned, as they will provide a nice and easy, time-saving process for you. After you have completed the purchase of the domain and the hosting service, the next step is to upload the WordPress setup to the server where -as you will see in the next chapter- using providers like Bluehost can make things quick and simple.

To sign up with Bluehost follow these steps:

1. Visit bluehost.com

2. You should see an advert that shows you the $3.49 deal, Click *Get Started Now* button

3. You will land on a page that shows you the different plans available

select your plan

	basic	plus	pro
		most popular	
	normally $7.00	normally $10.00	normally $33.00
	$3.49* per month	$5.95* per month	$13.95* per month
	select	select	select
websites	1	10	unlimited
website space	50 GB	150 GB	unmetered
bandwidth	unmetered	unmetered	unmetered
performance	Standard	Standard	High Performance
included domains	1	1	1
parked domains	5	20	unlimited
sub domains	25	50	unlimited
email accounts	5	100	unlimited
email storage	100 MB per account	500 MB per account	unlimited
marketing offers	—	$150 included	$300 included
	select	over $24/yr in extras	over $180/yr in extras
		Global CDN	Global CDN
		1 SpamExperts	2 SpamExperts
			1 SSL
		select	1 Dedicated IP
			1 Domain Privacy
			SiteBackup Pro
			select

4. Select the plan that is most suitable for your needs.

You have the option between a basic (£3.49), Plus ($5.95) or Pro plan ($13.95). I recommend going with the most basic plan. It gives you all you require whilst keeping your start-up costs low. You can always upgrade later if necessary.

However, bear in mind that you would have to pay for the package upfront. Assuming that you want to sign-up for 36 months, this would work out to a total of $125.64. If you want to go only for a 12-month package, then the cost goes up to $4.95 per month and you must pay $59.40 upfront. The third option is for a 24-month package of $3.95 per month and you have to pay $94.80 upfront.

So, decide whether you are committed and can also afford to pay the 36-month package of $125, which of course works out cheaper in the long-run, or whether you want to go for a 24-month or even just a 12-month package. Also, these prices are **excluding** tax.

package information

Account Plan		Basic 12 month $4.95/mo.		Basic 24 month $3.95/mo.	o	Basic 36 month $3.49/mo.
Hosting Price	$125.64 ($3.49 for 36 months)					
Setup Fee	Free					

There are also a few extras available like; 'Constant Contact' which is an email marketing service, 'Site Backup Pro' which backs-up your sites' files, 'Search Engine Jumpstart' signs you up to *SoloSEO* which places your site in search engines and helps you with SEO, then you have the final extra which is *SiteLock* which is a security service for your website.

Constant Contact	☑ - $10 per month for first 6 months (normally $20 per month)
	More information
Site Backup Pro	☑ - $1.99 per month (Billed to end of hosting term)
	More information
Search Engine Jumpstart	☑ - $1.25 per month (Billed annually at $14.99/yr)
	More information
SiteLock Security - Find	☑ - $1.99 per month (Billed annually at $23.88/yr)
	More information
Tax	$25.13
Total	$150.77

My advice would be to not sign up to any of these services. There are various free plugins that will do the same functions just as well, or better. Stick around for the last chapter where I will give you a list of my favourite 6 plugins.

Also for the SEO (search engine optimization) side of things, you can download my SEO guide (http://amzn.to/21HWFWb) that will teach you how to beat all your competition and rank on top. More on my SEO guide in a second.

5. Choose your domain name.

If you **don't have one**, type in your desired domain name on the box on the left. (If you already have a domain name, skip.

Picking a domain name is a simple task but can have a massive impact in the success and popularity of your website.

Basic SEO (search engine optimization) teaches you should include the name of the brand or service you want people to search for in your domain name.

For example:

If I am running a blog about my love for pets my domain could possibly be 'www.felixpetlover.com' since this includes the keywords 'pet lovers' and are most likely going to searched by interested visitors.

24

It is important to take this into consideration, because when people search for you or your service on popular search engines, you will have a higher probability of appearing high-up on the results if you have the main keywords of the search in your domain name. This will result in a larger number of people visiting your website, being involved with your blog, or purchasing your service/product.

Moment of Thought: Think about how many times you click through more than 2 pages on Google, or if you even go down the entire first page when searching for something. Not too often, right? So, really mull over the importance of getting your website as high up as possible!

Apart from assisting you in optimizing your search-engine ranking, choosing the right domain name that easily relates to you will make it easier for people to remember your website, as well as aid in building your brand.

Of course, including it in your domain name is just one of the many vital strategies you must use if you want your site to succeed. To aid you with this, I have created a guide that will teach you those strategies.

If you wish to learn more in regard to SEO (strongly recommended), download my **#1 Best-Selling**, step-by-step guide:

"SEO: Easy Search Engine Optimization For Beginners, Your Step-By-Step Guide to a Sky-High Search Engine Ranking and Never Ending Traffic".

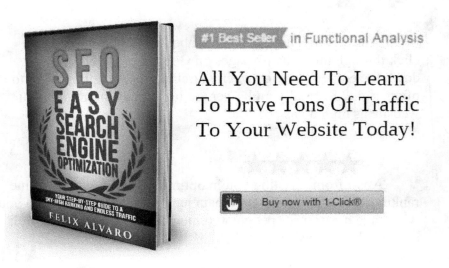

I would even urge you to buy this guide before actually launching your site, as it will teach you a number of tactics you should be applying on the backend of your site to really give yourself a big advantage over your competitors and to drive tons of traffic to your new site.

Please visit http://amzn.to/21HWFWb to download this must-have guide!

Moving on, once you have decided on a domain to your liking, think about how you want to end it. In the US, the majority of domains end with '.com' but there are other availabilities. For example, '.us', but I would recommend keeping it simple and professional. Go with '.com,' '.co.uk,' '.net,' or even '.org' if you are running an organization.

If you are in the UK, you won't see '.co.uk' available on bluehost's list, I would advise you in that case, to purchase your domain from a registrar like GoDaddy and transfer it to Bluehost using an *EPP Authorization Code*. I will be taking you step-by-step through this process below.

6. Check availability and complete your registration by entering your personal information. (Also, if your chosen domain name is not available, bluehost will give you alternative options.)

sign up - congratulations!

The domain you have requested, **testdomainname1223.com**, is available.

account information

All fields are required unless otherwise noted.

First Name	
Last Name	
(optional) Business Name	
Country	United States ▼
Street Address	
City	
State	Please select a state ▼
ZIP Code	
Phone Number	(123) 456-7890 Ext
	Use an international number
*E-mail Address	
	*Your receipt will be sent to this address.

7. If you **already have a domain**, enter it in the box on the right and then also fill in your personal information.

8. You will then have to verify ownership of this domain name by signing into your internet domain registrar (for example; GoDaddy.com) and copying your unique *EPP Authorization Code* for the selected domain name.

EPP Authorization Code transfer for GoDaddy:

- Visit Godaddy.ccom
- Click '*Domains*'

- Select the relevant domain from the list and click on '*Domain Settings*'

- Scroll down to '*Additional Settings*'

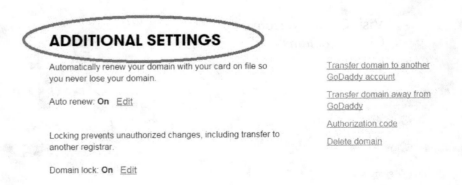

- On *'Domain Lock'* Click *'Edit'* and turn it off

| Domain lock: **On** ⬤ | Domain lock: **Off** ⬤ |

- Click on *'Authorization Code'*

ADDITIONAL SETTINGS

Automatically renew your domain with your card on file so you never lose your domain.

Auto renew: **On** Edit

Locking prevents unauthorized changes, including transfer to another registrar.

Transfer domain to another GoDaddy account

Transfer domain away from GoDaddy

 Authorization code

Delete domain

- GoDaddy will send you an email with your Authorization Code

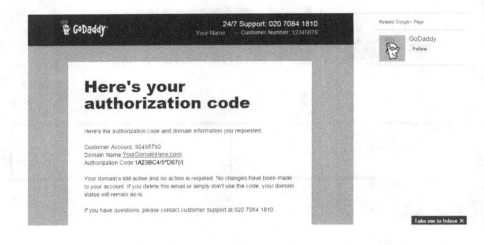

- Go to you Bluehost page
- Under the 'Domains' section, Click 'Transfer Domain'
- Enter the URL and Click Continue
- Enter the Authorization Code that GoDaddy sent you
- You receive another code by email which you must also enter here
- Select 'Use our nameservers'
- Select 'Automatically renew'
- Select 'Use Profile Information'
- Tick the box to agree to the Domain Registration Agreement
- Select the time period you want to renew your domain for, and add to basket
- Pay the renewal fee
- GoDaddy will send you an email asking if you want to accept or cancel the transfer
- Simply visit your GoDaddy account and under the Domains tab, Click on Transfers and then click Accept for the relevant domain name

- You are done!

9. Done!

We are making progress!

Now that you have purchased a domain and hosting server plan, let us proceed!

In next chapter, we will cover how to synchronize WordPress with the recently acquired domain and hosting server and then we will move onto to the set-up of your 'physical' website.

Chapter Three: Installing WordPress

Now we need to give your website a backbone...

In this chapter, we will begin by installing WordPress and linking it to your domain name. In the previous chapter, I pointed out that having a good service like Bluehost can truly make your life easier, as you will now see.

There are two ways of installing WordPress. I will teach you both ways so you have options; however, one is much, much easier than the other. I want you to reassure that if you took another route with installation I am still able to provide some guidance and assistance, so bear with me.

Firstly, we have the **1-click installation**:

If you followed my advice (as I hope you did!) you would have set up your website using bluehost.com. As I stated before, their service works best when putting a website together. With Bluehost we can actually install WordPress with the click of a button.

I will lay it out to you as simply as possible:

1. Log in to your Bluehost account
2. Go to your control-panel page

3. You should see a 'WordPress' icon, under the *Website Builders* section. Click it.

4. This will take you to the MOJO marketplace page. Click on *'Install Now'*

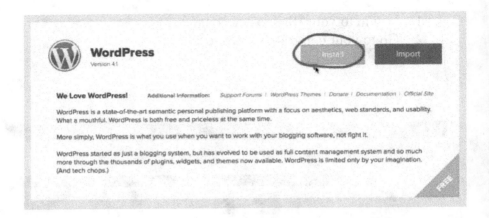

5. Select the domain name from the drop-down menu (If you bought your domain name from a different registrar like GoDaddy, you will have to firstly verify your domain name with your EPP Auth Code as I showed you previously, otherwise it won't appear here). Then Click *'Check Domain'*.

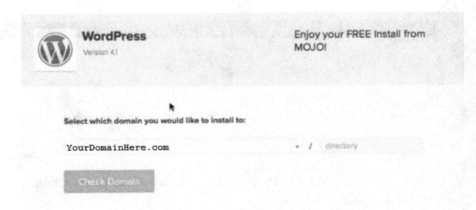

6. Once checked, Click on '*Show advanced options*'

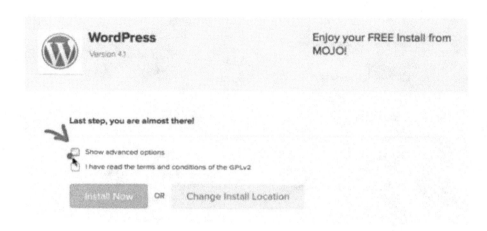

7. Choose your site name and most importantly, your **Admin-Username** and **Password**. You will need these to have access your WordPress Dashboard and to begin creating your site.

    TIP: You can either go with the automatically generated password or you can choose your own, just be sure to choose a secure password.

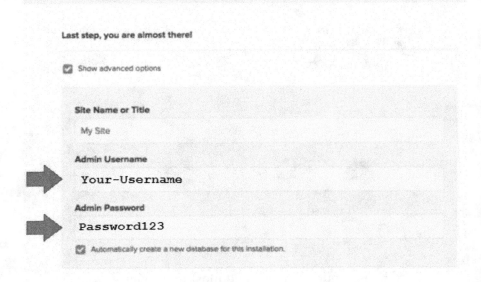

8. Ensure that the box '*Automatically create a new database for this installation*' is selected, then select the box to confirm that you agree with the Terms & Conditions and Click '*Install Now*'

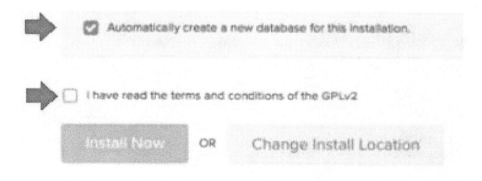

9. Wait a few minutes whilst WordPress completes the installation

Your install is underway!

10. Once complete, Click on *'View Credentials'*

Your install is complete!   View Credentials

11. This will then show you all your login details, including the admin-link you need to visit to get access to your site, your username and password.

Congratulations on the installation of your new WordPress site! **Your login information is below.**

Step 1. Access your New WordPress site

URL: http://www.YourDomainHere.com
Admin URL: http://www.YourDomainHere.com/wp-admin
Username: Your-Username
Password: Password123

12. Visit the Admin URL and attempt to login using the username and password you selected

13. TADA! You should get access to your new website!

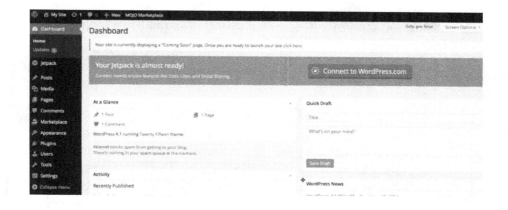

The second method is the **manual installation**: (If you used the 1-click installation, simply skip to Chapter 4)

If you are using a hosting service where there is no 1-click installation feature you can then install it manually, which is explained below:

1. Download WordPress using this link: http://wordpress.org/download - Create a new folder on your PC desktop and unzip the WordPress software in it
2. Upload the WordPress files using FTP (File Transfer Protocol). Log in to your hosting FTP which can be accessed by downloading 'FileZilla.' Using FileZilla, you get a drag-and-drop feature to move the files. The FTP address is usually 'ftp.yourdomain.com'. The username and password are the same as what you used to register to your host
3. Now construct a MySQL database and username through cPanel. <u>Be sure to remember the database name, the username, and the password, as you will need it later</u>! After adding the user with the database, select 'All Privileges' then 'Make Changes' to complete this step
4. Go back to your files and look for a file with the name '*wp-config-sample.php*' and rename that file as '*wp-config.php*'. Be sure to delete the '*wp-config-sample.php*' from FileZilla and upload the '*wp-config.php*' to it!
5. This next step is why you needed to remember the previous information. Now open that file (*wp-config.php*) with notepad, for instance, and fill in the following:
   - define('DB_NAME', 'database_name_here'); = Your database name
   - define('DB_USER', 'username_here'); =Your hosting username

- define('DB_PASSWORD', 'password_here'); = Your hosting password

6. After this, scroll down a bit until you find the entire section of define('AUTH_KEY', 'put your unique phrase here');. There should be eight lines total of this section. This is where you put your security key, which can be found in an https link a few lines up. Copy the link and paste it to a browser to get your security key. Copy the key and paste it back into the file through the entire section of 'put your unique phrase here'.

7. Scroll down once more to find $table_prefix = 'wp_';. Change the wp_ part with either added numbers or an extra letter (for example: wp_35) to prevent an easy attack from hackers! And Save the file

8. Go to yourwebsitedomainhere.com/wp-admin/install.php

9. You should see a WordPress page with a form to fill in. Fill it in and we are done!

Phew! You made it through the manual installation. That's an accomplishment! You can see why the 1-click installation is the quickest, easiest option. Sometimes knowing you put in the extra work to create your website makes it feel as though you passed an amazing feat.

In this chapter, we covered the two ways of synchronizing WordPress with your domain and server. You now have an actual website to begin building! With installation finished, it is time to continue on with your website design!

In the next chapter, I will show you how to add a touch of your personality to your website through the use of themes!

Chapter Four: Website Make-over!

Now that we have our domain name and hosting server all synchronized to WordPress, all we have to do now is begin giving colour, shape, and personality to our website!

Once you log in to your WordPress domain, you will see the basic outlay of your website with the preloaded theme. Even though the current theme presented is cleanly put together, I am sure you are eager to add your own touch. Now is the chance to create something unique and different!

There are thousands upon thousands of fully-customizable themes available for you to choose from and upload to your website. To find such themes, follow the simple steps I have laid-out for you below:

1. Log in to your Dashboard

This is where you control the appearance and features of your website. At first glance, it may look like a nightmare! You have all these buttons and unfamiliar terms, but I promise you the navigation is easier than it seems. Just after a few hours of playing around and practice you will have full grasp of how everything works. For now, all we want to do is change the theme of our website. As we move forward I will show you how it's done.

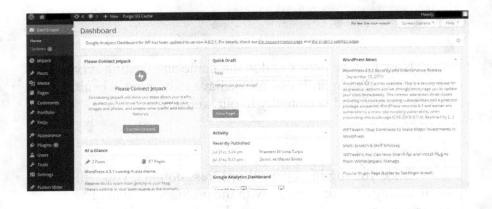

2. Choosing a Free Theme!

On the Dashboard page (which is located on the top left of your WordPress website page) you should see an option named 'Appearance' with a little paint brush on it. Click on it, and you will see the 'Themes' option appears below. Click on that next.

Here you have access to over 1,000 different themes to suit all tastes. Themes vary between quirky to more simple and smooth ones. You can search through the themes using keywords or filters to find a theme that fits your desires. This may take a while, but I recommend going through a few to find that one that not only matches what you want, but is also relevant to the viewing audience. Remember, they will be judging by the first look and layout of your website, so make sure to spend some time selecting what is appropriate and enticing to the viewer.

It is extremely wise to be confident in selecting a theme that is labelled as 'responsive' because they will have the best layout for mobiles and other devices as well. This is especially important if your target audience is towards a younger age group since they are more likely to access your website from their mobile-phone rather than a PC. Keep that in mind!

If the themes offered do not meet your needs you can also head down to www.themeforest.net where you can purchase additional themes. They have thousands of portfolios of themes that all vary in price. This will also provide you with something more unique in comparison to the free-ones; nevertheless, consider both and decide on what is best for you and your audience.

3. Finally: Installing the Theme

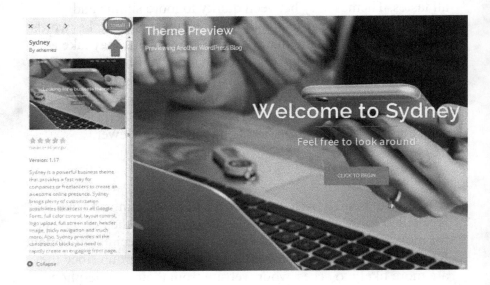

Once you have decided on the perfect theme, it is time to install it! All you have to do is click 'install' and then click on 'Activate' to get it completely installed.

Also, do not worry if you have already added content to your website! Installing a theme will not delete any pages, posts, or any content what-so-ever. You can always change a theme if you sense a change of taste in your viewing audience, if you are launching a new product or idea, or if you just want to give a new appearance to your website.

With your theme updated, you can now begin adding content to your website, if you have not done so already. In the next chapter, you will learn how to add pages and content to your website!

Chapter Five: Filling your Website with Pages and Content

You are getting even closer to your finished website! Now that it has a personality and design, we want to begin adding pages with amazing content for our viewing visitors to enjoy.

I prefer to begin with an 'About me' page where I talk about myself, what I do, and the aim for the website or blog. I would highly recommend that you start with the same.

Hot Tip: It is important to note that having an 'About me/us' page also boosts your SEO rank and helps push you up higher on the results pages. This is due to Google or other search engines seeing your website as credible, professional and relevant to the searched term, therefore bringing it up first for people to see it.

So how do you **add a page**? This is incredibly simple to do.

1. Go back to the Dashboard to see a 'Pages' option located two links above 'Appearance.' Once you have selected 'Pages' you will get the drop- down menu options where you should select 'Add new.'
2. Then you should get a new page that looks like a word or a text document. At the top, you can select the title of the page, the link to the page (for example: yourwebsite.com/about_me –which, by the way, is super important for SEO and how users find your page) and of course the option to add any text or images.
3. Be sure to click 'Preview' on the right to see how everything is going to look, then click 'Publish' once you are happy with everything. Alternatively, you can also choose 'Save Draft' if you want to come back to it later!

Our page is now complete but, if you don't add it to the menu, our visitors will not be able to find it unless they have the direct link, (yourwebstie.com/about_me). Therefore, it is important to add it to the menu for easy access to the page.

To **add a page to the menu**, we want to do the following:

1. On the Dashboard, you want to select 'Appearance' once again
2. This time select 'Menus' located three places below 'Themes'
3. On the page that opens we should then get a little table on the left that has 'Most recent,' 'View All,' and 'Search.' You want to be on 'Most recent' as this should show us the page we just created
4. Select that relevant page - in this example we should see 'About Me' (or whatever title you gave)- by clicking the box
5. Click 'Add to Menu'
6. Under *Menu Structure,* drag and organize the layout of the menu, I recommend making 'About me' one of the first pages on the menu. You can also make a page a drop-down page, by dragging in on top of the menu. Like the picture below where I have made the 'Our Mission' and 'Who We Are' pages *sub items* of the 'About Us' page.

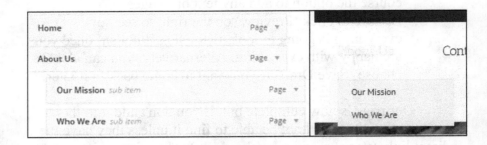

7. Finally, under *Menu Settings* make sure to click '*Home Page Header Menu,*' then press 'SAVE MENU' on the right.

Hot Tip: With some of the themes accessible on WordPress, you receive these pre-loaded side bars (widgets) that may not be so appealing.

However, removing them is quite simple, and I will quickly explain how to do so:

1. On the Dashboard click our lovely 'Appearance' link
2. This time on the menu you want to select 'Widgets'
3. Here you can remove sidebars by click the arrow next each one and <u>clicking</u> *Remove*
4. To add a new one, just drag one from the *Available Widgets* and drop in a particular sidebar

Also: For all my Sensei coding masters, you also have an option to add HTML code using a text box, but if you are just starting, don't even bother with that!

Now on to the content...

If you are choosing to run a blog, then the next step for you should be creating new 'Posts.' To add a new post all you do is:

1. Open our lovely Dashboard once more!
2. Two options below you will see *Posts,* select that
3. You can then select *'Add New'* on the top-left

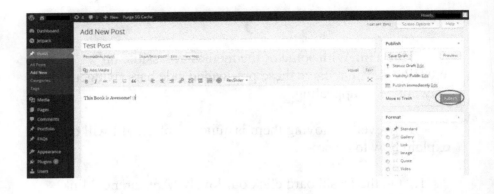

One thing I will mention is the *Categories* feature. When you are adding posts, you have the option of selecting particular categories to group similar posts on your website or, more importantly, your blog. You can create new categories by simply <u>clicking</u> the '*Posts*' link and then choosing '*categories*' below that.

Here, you can choose a category name (for example 'Blog') and <u>click</u> '*Add new category*' at the bottom of the page. From here, you have the opportunity to select this category every time you want to make a post on your 'Blog' (Just select the 'Blog' category at the bottom right of the new posts page). Keeping everything in order and separating posts in accordance to their topics will give your blog a professional and organized touch.

In addition, when you add posts and content you can allow people to comment on the posts and on the pages. If you do not want people to do so (which is understandable), I will show how to do that:

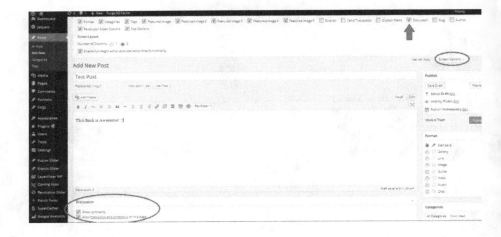

1. When you are writing a new page, or want to add a new post to one of your informative categories we just created, you will get a small drop-down menu under *'Screen Options' on* the top right of both pages. Click on that.

2. Then you will get a few boxes with a couple of different options. What we want to do is click the 'Discussions' box before scrolling down the page where below the text-box you will see two options: *'Allow Comments'* and *'Allow trackbacks...'*

3. Ignore the latter and just un-click the *Allow Comments'* box and you are done!

   If you wish to **disable comments on all pages** by default, then this is what you do:

1. Go on the Dashboard home

2. Hover your mouse over the 'Settings' link and select 'Discussion'

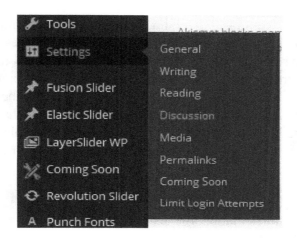

3. Then under 'Default article settings' right at the top, simply <u>unselect</u> the 'Allow people to post comments on new article'

4. Go to the bottom of the page and click 'Save Changes'- Done!

One more SEO tip:

I said I wouldn't talk about SEO anymore, but I really want you to have a correctly optimized website. So here goes one more tip; Another powerful set of tools you can use to boost the search rank of your website are *Titles* and *Taglines*. What this will do is give your website a "title" on the search engine (link the title to whatever people are searching). I would recommend that you select something that is relevant to you and what people are likely to search if they are looking for you, like your name or business-name. For instance, I may put "Felix". With the tagline, you may simply choose to put your slogan or the word 'blog', or the topic that relates to you. Just make sure to always choose 'searchable' titles and taglines that people actually search for. I advise to not write anything extreme or odd.

For more on the importance of keyword optimization and how to find the best keywords to rank for, download my step-by-step SEO guide by visiting; http://amzn.to/21HWFWb

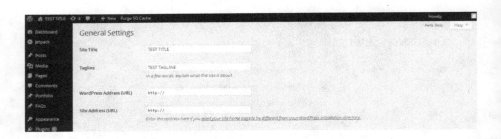

To add a Title and Tagline go to the Dashboard, select *Settings,* and you should see a small form asking for a *Site Title* and *Tagline*. Add those before selecting '*Save Changes*' at the bottom of the page.

Take a moment to appreciate your progress! In this chapter, you have just learned how to add pages and how to fill them with content for your readers to enjoy. In the upcoming chapter, you will learn about the power of Plugins, and how a simple touch of a button can add amazing features to your website... Your website is inching closer to completion!

Chapter Six: Power of WordPress - Plugins and much more!

Earlier on in the book, I mentioned that one of the beautiful aspects of WordPress is the way you can <u>easily</u> add amazing features to your website. Whereas other platforms would require coding skills and hours of struggling. The reason for this effortless process is due to the use of Plugins and widgets, which is what we will cover in this chapter.

Plugins are extensions that enable you to simply add pre-made features to your website. Similar to adding an app to your smart-phone. For instance, if you want to add a box where someone could send you a message so it comes straight to an email of your choice, you can do it at the click of a button.

Widgets are also pre-designed functions that will work hand-in-hand with your plugins and coding. They are the part of a plugin that would actually be displayed on your web-page so they don't actually have a functionality on their own. With the message box example, the function of the message being sent and received would be the plugin. The physical box on the page would be the widget that you can move around. (To add widgets simply refer back to the last chapter, where I explained how to remove the widget sidebars that come pre-loaded with certain themes.)

To make this even better you have a wide range of plugins and widgets at your disposal to choose from for ABSOLUTELY FREE! So, you can add exceptionally professional features to your website to increase the credibility and quality of your brand. This would have cost you a fortune to have done a few years back (though do remember it can still cost a fortune today if you're not careful!).

Moving on, let me explain how to get these amazing Plugins!

Here you go:

1. On your dashboard, you should see a lovely little button with the words *Plugins*
2. Select it and then select 'Add new'
3. Search whatever you want and choose from over 25,000 different plugins available at your finger-tips!

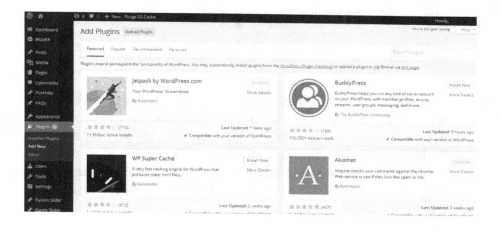

BUT WAIT!!!

Before you go on a plugin-marathon and install every single plugin out there I want to give you some words of wisdom. I call this my…

Three Rules for Plugin Success and Efficiency;

1. Updating, updating, updating!!

Just as your mobile device or your PC needs continuous updating of software to keep up with the malware and viruses, your site also needs its plugins to be updated to prevent damage or theft of your data. So please, ensure that you update your plugins often, and if you are not using a particular plugin DELETE IT! You can still be attacked via deactivated plugins that are not up-to-date.

2. The number of plugins is pretty much irrelevant, sometimes.

Do not be concerned with having quite a few plugins running at the same time on your website. What is important is how well protected and well coded they are. Any gaps or mistakes in the coding can make your whole operation vulnerable. However, ensure -to the best of your ability- that there are no plugins that conflict with one another, since the more you have, the higher the risk of that happening.

3. Go for the highest rated and recommended plugins

There will certainly be times where a particular plugin appeals to you and you will want to quickly install it and try it out. However, be cautious of this as many can have poor coding and can leave behind digital footprint (leftover data) on your website. To minimize the risk of this, it is wise to go with popular plugins that have gained positive reviews, as well as having been created by established developers.

Amazing! You should now be ready to add some spectacular features to your site and just to give you some inspiration, I will present to you my,

Top 6 must-have plugins;

1. <u>W3 total Cache</u>

W3 Total Cache   Install Now

Easy Web Performance Optimization (WPO) using   More Details
caching: browser, page, object, database, minify and
content delivery network support.

By Frederick Townes

★ ★ ★ ★ ⯪ (2,588)   Last Updated: 1 month ago

1+ Million Active Installs   ✔ Compatible with your version of WordPress

This plugin has nearly reached one million installations and almost 2,500 reviews with a rating of 4.5 out of 5. So, what does it do to have this popularity? In a nutshell, it increases the speed that your website loads by up to 10xs! Yes, ten times! It's an absolute must-have! It will also boost your page rank and load time, which is great news if you are using a shared-server. Yet, this can be awfully difficult to set-up, so if you are not up for the challenge I would recommend having a look at 'Better WordPress Minify'. 'Better WordPress Minify' offers an easier option that also boosts the responsiveness of your site and is much easier to install. Nevertheless, W3 Total Cache is still one of my favourites.

2. Forget speed, let us talk about efficiency!

Back to my three favourite letters S.E.O., *WordPress SEO by Yoast* proves to be much more than a plugin since it turns your website into a cleverly optimized machine. This plugin has cool features like the optimization of title, descriptions and even individual posts in order to significantly enhance the ranking of your website on search engines.

3. **UpdraftPlus Backup & Restoration**

UpdraftPlus Backup and Restoration

Backup and restoration made easy. Complete
backups; manual or scheduled (backup to S3,
Dropbox, Google Drive, Rackspace, FTP, SFTP, email +
others).

By UpdraftPlus.Com, DavidAnderson

Install Now

More Details

★ ★ ★ ★ ★ (1,662)

500,000+ Active Installs

Last Updated: 2 days ago

✓ Compatible with your version of WordPress

This plugin is the Number #1 Backup Plugin on WordPress. It will enable you to store all your information safely at a click of a button. What makes it really cool for me, besides the simplicity to use, is that it allows users to easily setup automatic back-up schedules for their WordPress website and upload it to their DropBox, Google Drive, Microsoft OneDrive or even Amazon Cloud (and others). Restoration is also very simple, quick and convenient so this Plugin is a must!

4. MailPoet Newsletters

MailPoet grants you the ability to build your customer or fan base by sending out newsletters to your viewers. The plugin is quite easy to operate, making it a must if you want to build that relationship with your visitors. You also receive valuable features such as an 'automatic-send' that allows you to schedule delivery of newsletters, as well as providing you with statistics of how many people open the newsletters, how many clicks you get, and how many people have unsubscribed from your service. Absolutely brilliant!

5. Jetpack

Jetpack by WordPress.com
Your WordPress, Streamlined.
By Automattic

Installed

More Details

★★★★☆ (710)
1+ Million Active Installs

Last Updated: 1 week ago
✓ Compatible with your version of WordPress

There are similar plugins to Jetpack, but this particular one is essential. Jetpack allows you to add 'mini-plugins' in order to improve the performance and usability of your website. The mini-plugins vary between adding Google+ profiles to adding a contact form for your 'contact us' page!

6. Google Analytics by Yoast

Google Analytics by Yoast   Installed

Track your WordPress site easily with the latest   More Details
tracking codes and lots added data for search result
pages and error pages.

By Team Yoast

★ ★ ★ ★ ☆ (324)   Last Updated: 3 months ago
1+ Million Active Installs   ✓ Compatible with your version of WordPress

This one is an absolute must. As they say, "Numbers don't lie", and this Plugin will show you the factual performance of your website. Google Analytics by Yoast will provide you with in-depth, but easy to read reports and graphs of your site's performance including in-depth visitor monitoring, downloads, clicks and links tracking, reports of visitor location and much more. All accessible from your WordPress Dashboard! Simply create a Google Analytics account (Gmail account), follow some simple set-up steps and you are good to go!

There you have my top six, must have, plugins. I hope you enjoyed that list and received some value from it. Like I mentioned before, there are thousands of plugins to choose from, just ensure that they are high- quality and valuable for your site!

Now that you have read through the book I believe you are fully equipped to launch an absolutely outstanding website or blog! Make sure to use this book as a guide if you are ever stuck and be sure to put what you have learned into practice right away.

If you haven't already done so, remember to download my SEO guide which goes into detail on how to better optimize your website or blog for search engines, giving you a huge advantage over your competition and placing your blog in front of many, many more people. The learning never stops! Please visit; http://amzn.to/21HWFWb to download now!

Turn to the next page for a quick recap on what we covered in this book!

Here is a quick recap of what we covered in case you need a refresher on a certain step:

1. You now have an understanding of WordPress and how it operates
2. You learned how to wisely select the right domain name and hosting server
3. You learned how to synchronize it with WordPress
4. You learned how to add personality to a webpage through the use of themes
5. You learned how to add pages and awesome content to a website
6. You also learned the Power of WordPress through the use of Plugins and much more!

Turn to the next page to gain access to a free video course and to also see my other best-selling books part of this series!

Before You Go

I hope you have enjoyed this book and have benefited immensely from reading it. I made it my goal to offer value -and to give you the necessary confidence to begin creating a website with WordPress- to the best of my ability. I am glad that you are reading this far down.

Also, whether this captured your interest or not, I would really appreciate your reviews and your feedback. If you really enjoyed this book, then feel free to share it so other people may also profit from this information. Tell all your friends! (Or not, but I will be saddened) Lol!

To leave a review:

Please visit http://amzn.to/1KwgYhH

In case you missed it, here are some of my other awesome, **best-selling** books!

Here Are Other Books Our Readers Loved!

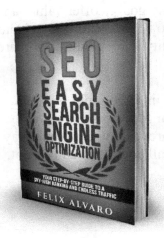

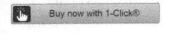

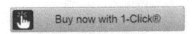

http://amzn.to/1mBhUYM

Best Seller in Popular Counting & Numeration

Learn Python Programming Today With This Easy, Step-By-Step Guide!

Buy now with 1-Click®

http://amzn.to/1WOBiy2

NEW

Learn Java Programming Today With This Easy, Step-By-Step Guide!

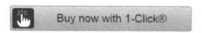
Buy now with 1-Click®

http://amzn.to/1WTgUw0

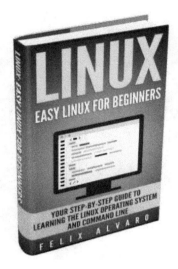

Learn The Linux Operating System and Command Line Today!

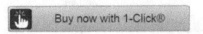

Buy now with 1-Click®

http://amzn.to/1QzQPkY

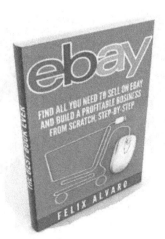

Launch Your Own Profitable eBay Business- Learn Everything You Need to Know to Get Started Today!

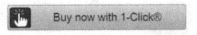

Buy now with 1-Click®

http://amzn.to/1R1vnCP

Learn C Programming Today With This Easy, Step-By-Step Guide

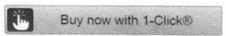

http://amzn.to/1WI6fHu

Learn R Programming With This Easy, Step-By-Step Guide

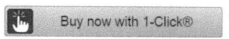

http://amzn.to/24XxoLM

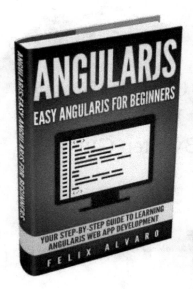

Learn AngularJS Web-App Developing Today With This Easy, Step-By-Step Guide

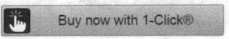

Finally, you can also send me an email if you have any questions, feedback or just want to say hello! (I do reply!) My email address is; (Felix_Alvaro@mail.com)

I thank you once again and God bless!

Felix Alvaro

www.ingramcontent.com/pod-product-compliance
Lightning Source LLC
Chambersburg PA
CBHW061030050326
40689CB00012B/2749